The Ultimate Sous Vide Guide: 50 Perfect Dishes

By: Kelly Johnson

Table of Contents

- Sous Vide Ribeye Steak
- Sous Vide Chicken Breast
- Sous Vide Salmon
- Sous Vide Pork Tenderloin
- Sous Vide Lamb Chops
- Sous Vide Shrimp
- Sous Vide Duck Breast
- Sous Vide Filet Mignon
- Sous Vide Short Ribs
- Sous Vide Lobster Tail
- Sous Vide Chicken Thighs
- Sous Vide Pork Belly
- Sous Vide Prime Rib
- Sous Vide Trout
- SousVide Beef Tenderloin
- Sous Vide Swordfish
- Sous Vide Veal Chops
- Sous Vide Beef Brisket
- Sous Vide Vegetables Medley
- Sous Vide Asparagus
- Sous Vide Potatoes
- Sous Vide Carrots
- Sous Vide Sweet Potatoes
- Sous Vide Corn on the Cob
- Sous Vide Eggs (Soft/Hard Boiled)
- Sous Vide Scallops
- Sous Vide Cheesecake
- Sous Vide Ribs
- Sous Vide Chicken Wings
- Sous Vide Brisket
- Sous Vide Steak Frites
- Sous Vide Crab Cakes
- Sous Vide Pork Chops
- Sous Vide Beef Wellington
- Sous Vide Banana Bread

- Sous Vide Oysters
- Sous Vide Fried Chicken
- Sous Vide Meatballs
- Sous Vide Venison
- Sous Vide Duck Confit
- Sous Vide Pork Ribs
- Sous Vide Gnocchi
- Sous Vide Pork Ragu
- Sous Vide Eggplant Parmesan
- Sous Vide Beef Bolognese
- Sous Vide Caramelized Onions
- Sous Vide Tofu
- Sous Vide Grilled Cheese Sandwich
- Sous Vide Risotto
- Sous Vide Apple Pie

Sous Vide Ribeye Steak

Ingredients:

- 2 ribeye steaks (1.5 inches thick)
- Salt and pepper to taste
- 2 cloves garlic, crushed
- 2 sprigs fresh rosemary
- 1 tbsp olive oil

Instructions:

1. Preheat sous vide water bath to 54°C (130°F) for medium-rare.
2. Season ribeye steaks with salt and pepper, and place garlic and rosemary in the bag.
3. Vacuum seal the steaks and cook in the water bath for 1.5 to 2 hours.
4. After cooking, remove the steaks and pat them dry with paper towels.
5. Heat olive oil in a skillet over high heat and sear each steak for 1-2 minutes on each side to create a crust.
6. Let rest for a few minutes, then slice and serve.

Sous Vide Chicken Breast

Ingredients:

- 2 chicken breasts (boneless, skinless)
- Salt and pepper to taste
- 1 tbsp olive oil or butter
- 1 sprig rosemary or thyme (optional)

Instructions:

1. Preheat sous vide water bath to 64°C (147°F).
2. Season chicken breasts with salt, pepper, and olive oil or butter.
3. Vacuum seal the chicken breasts with herbs if desired.
4. Cook for 1.5 to 2 hours.
5. Once done, remove from the bag, pat dry, and sear in a hot skillet for 1-2 minutes per side for a crispy exterior.
6. Slice and serve with your favorite sides.

Sous Vide Salmon

Ingredients:

- 2 salmon fillets (skin-on)
- Salt and pepper to taste
- 1 tbsp olive oil or butter
- Lemon slices (optional)
- Fresh dill or herbs (optional)

Instructions:

1. Preheat sous vide water bath to 50°C (122°F) for delicate, tender salmon.
2. Season salmon fillets with salt and pepper, and add olive oil or butter. Optionally, include lemon slices and herbs in the bag.
3. Vacuum seal and cook for 45 minutes to 1 hour.
4. After cooking, carefully remove from the bag and serve with a drizzle of olive oil, fresh herbs, or lemon wedges.

Sous Vide Pork Tenderloin

Ingredients:

- 1 pork tenderloin (about 500g)
- Salt and pepper to taste
- 2 cloves garlic, crushed
- 1 tbsp olive oil or butter
- 1 sprig rosemary or thyme

Instructions:

1. Preheat sous vide water bath to 63°C (145°F).
2. Season the pork tenderloin with salt, pepper, and garlic. Add herbs and vacuum seal.
3. Cook for 2 to 3 hours in the water bath.
4. Once done, remove from the bag, pat dry, and sear in a hot pan with olive oil or butter for 2-3 minutes per side.
5. Slice and serve with roasted vegetables or mashed potatoes.

Sous Vide Lamb Chops

Ingredients:

- 4 lamb chops
- Salt and pepper to taste
- 2 cloves garlic, crushed
- 1 tbsp olive oil or butter
- 2 sprigs fresh rosemary

Instructions:

1. Preheat sous vide water bath to 57°C (135°F) for medium-rare lamb.
2. Season lamb chops with salt and pepper, and add garlic and rosemary.
3. Vacuum seal the lamb chops and cook for 1.5 to 2 hours.
4. Remove from the bag, pat dry, and sear in a hot skillet for 1-2 minutes per side.
5. Let rest briefly, then serve with mint sauce or your favorite sides.

Sous Vide Shrimp

Ingredients:

- 12 large shrimp, peeled and deveined
- 2 tbsp olive oil or butter
- 1 clove garlic, minced
- Salt and pepper to taste
- Lemon zest (optional)

Instructions:

1. Preheat sous vide water bath to 60°C (140°F).
2. Season shrimp with olive oil, garlic, salt, pepper, and lemon zest.
3. Vacuum seal and cook for 30-45 minutes.
4. Once done, remove from the bag and serve with cocktail sauce, pasta, or over a salad.

Sous Vide Duck Breast

Ingredients:

- 2 duck breasts (skin-on)
- Salt and pepper to taste
- 1 sprig rosemary (optional)
- 1 tbsp olive oil or butter

Instructions:

1. Preheat sous vide water bath to 58°C (136°F).
2. Score the duck skin in a crosshatch pattern, season with salt and pepper, and add rosemary (optional).
3. Vacuum seal the duck breasts and cook for 2 to 3 hours.
4. After cooking, remove from the bag, pat dry, and sear the skin side in a hot pan with olive oil or butter for 2-3 minutes to crisp up the skin.
5. Slice and serve with a berry sauce or sautéed greens.

Sous Vide Filet Mignon

Ingredients:

- 2 filet mignon steaks
- Salt and pepper to taste
- 2 tbsp olive oil or butter
- 1 sprig fresh thyme or rosemary

Instructions:

1. Preheat sous vide water bath to 54°C (130°F) for medium-rare.
2. Season the steaks with salt and pepper, then vacuum seal with thyme or rosemary.
3. Cook for 1.5 to 2 hours in the water bath.
4. After cooking, remove from the bag, pat dry, and sear in a hot skillet for 1-2 minutes per side for a golden crust.
5. Let the steaks rest before serving.

Sous Vide Short Ribs

Ingredients:

- 2-3 short ribs (bone-in)
- Salt and pepper to taste
- 2 cloves garlic, minced
- 1 tbsp olive oil
- 1 cup beef broth
- 1 tbsp soy sauce

Instructions:

1. Preheat sous vide water bath to 65°C (149°F).
2. Season the short ribs with salt, pepper, and garlic, then vacuum seal with broth and soy sauce.
3. Cook for 24 hours in the water bath for tender, fall-off-the-bone ribs.
4. After cooking, remove from the bag and sear the short ribs in a hot pan with olive oil for 2-3 minutes per side.
5. Serve with mashed potatoes or over polenta.

Sous Vide Lobster Tail

Ingredients:

- 2 lobster tails
- 2 tbsp butter
- 1 clove garlic, minced
- 1 tbsp lemon juice
- Salt and pepper to taste

Instructions:

1. Preheat the sous vide water bath to 60°C (140°F).
2. Using kitchen scissors, cut the top of the lobster shell down the center, exposing the meat.
3. Season lobster with salt, pepper, garlic, butter, and lemon juice.
4. Vacuum seal the lobster tails in a bag.
5. Cook in the water bath for 45-60 minutes.
6. After cooking, remove the lobster from the bag and sear the meat for 1-2 minutes in a hot pan for a golden finish.

Sous Vide Chicken Thighs

Ingredients:

- 4 bone-in, skin-on chicken thighs
- 1 tbsp olive oil
- 2 cloves garlic, minced
- 1 tsp paprika
- 1 tsp thyme
- Salt and pepper to taste

Instructions:

1. Preheat the sous vide water bath to 68°C (155°F).
2. Season the chicken thighs with olive oil, garlic, paprika, thyme, salt, and pepper.
3. Vacuum seal the chicken thighs.
4. Cook in the water bath for 1.5 to 2 hours.
5. After cooking, remove from the bag and sear in a hot skillet for 2-3 minutes per side to crisp the skin.

Sous Vide Pork Belly

Ingredients:

- 1kg pork belly
- 1 tbsp olive oil
- 2 tbsp soy sauce
- 1 tbsp honey
- 2 cloves garlic, minced
- Salt and pepper to taste

Instructions:

1. Preheat the sous vide water bath to 68°C (155°F).
2. Rub the pork belly with salt, pepper, garlic, olive oil, soy sauce, and honey.
3. Vacuum seal the pork belly.
4. Cook for 24 hours in the water bath.
5. After cooking, remove from the bag and sear the pork belly in a hot pan for 3-5 minutes on each side to get a crispy crust.

Sous Vide Prime Rib

Ingredients:

- 1 bone-in prime rib roast (about 1.5kg)
- 2 tbsp olive oil
- 4 cloves garlic, minced
- 1 tbsp fresh rosemary, chopped
- 1 tbsp fresh thyme, chopped
- Salt and pepper to taste

Instructions:

1. Preheat the sous vide water bath to 54°C (130°F) for medium-rare.
2. Rub the prime rib with olive oil, garlic, rosemary, thyme, salt, and pepper.
3. Vacuum seal the roast and cook in the water bath for 6-8 hours.
4. After cooking, remove from the bag and sear the prime rib in a hot pan for 1-2 minutes per side for a crispy crust.
5. Let rest before slicing and serving.

Sous Vide Trout

Ingredients:

- 2 trout fillets
- 2 tbsp olive oil
- 1 lemon, sliced
- 1 tsp fresh dill
- Salt and pepper to taste

Instructions:

1. Preheat the sous vide water bath to 54°C (130°F).
2. Season the trout fillets with salt, pepper, olive oil, dill, and place lemon slices on top.
3. Vacuum seal the trout fillets.
4. Cook in the water bath for 30-45 minutes.
5. After cooking, remove from the bag and serve immediately with your favorite side.

Sous Vide Beef Tenderloin

Ingredients:

- 2 beef tenderloin steaks
- 2 tbsp olive oil
- 2 cloves garlic, minced
- 1 tsp rosemary, chopped
- Salt and pepper to taste

Instructions:

1. Preheat the sous vide water bath to 54°C (130°F) for medium-rare.
2. Season the beef tenderloin steaks with olive oil, garlic, rosemary, salt, and pepper.
3. Vacuum seal the steaks.
4. Cook in the water bath for 1.5 to 2 hours.
5. After cooking, remove from the bag and sear in a hot skillet for 1-2 minutes per side.

Sous Vide Swordfish

Ingredients:

- 2 swordfish steaks
- 2 tbsp olive oil
- 1 lemon, juiced
- 1 tsp thyme
- Salt and pepper to taste

Instructions:

1. Preheat the sous vide water bath to 54°C (130°F).
2. Season swordfish steaks with olive oil, lemon juice, thyme, salt, and pepper.
3. Vacuum seal the steaks.
4. Cook in the water bath for 45-60 minutes.
5. After cooking, remove from the bag and sear for 1-2 minutes per side for a golden finish.

Sous Vide Veal Chops

Ingredients:

- 2 veal chops
- 1 tbsp olive oil
- 2 cloves garlic, minced
- 1 tbsp fresh rosemary, chopped
- Salt and pepper to taste

Instructions:

1. Preheat the sous vide water bath to 56°C (132°F) for medium-rare.
2. Season veal chops with olive oil, garlic, rosemary, salt, and pepper.
3. Vacuum seal the veal chops.
4. Cook in the water bath for 1.5 to 2 hours.
5. After cooking, remove from the bag and sear in a hot pan for 1-2 minutes per side to achieve a golden brown crust.

Sous Vide Beef Brisket

Ingredients:

- 1.5kg beef brisket
- 2 tbsp olive oil
- 1 tbsp smoked paprika
- 1 tbsp garlic powder
- 1 tbsp onion powder
- 1 tsp cumin
- Salt and pepper to taste

Instructions:

1. Preheat the sous vide water bath to 68°C (155°F).
2. Rub the brisket with olive oil, smoked paprika, garlic powder, onion powder, cumin, salt, and pepper.
3. Vacuum seal the brisket.
4. Cook in the water bath for 24 hours.
5. After cooking, remove from the bag and sear the brisket in a hot pan for 2-3 minutes per side.
6. Let rest before slicing and serving.

Sous Vide Vegetable Medley

Ingredients:

- 1 cup broccoli florets
- 1 cup cauliflower florets
- 1 cup carrots, sliced
- 1 cup bell peppers, sliced
- 1 tbsp olive oil
- 1 tsp garlic powder
- 1 tsp thyme
- Salt and pepper to taste

Instructions:

1. Preheat the sous vide water bath to 85°C (185°F).
2. Toss all vegetables in olive oil, garlic powder, thyme, salt, and pepper.
3. Vacuum seal the vegetable mixture in a bag.
4. Cook for 45-60 minutes in the water bath until tender.
5. Remove from the bag and serve immediately. Optionally, toss with a bit more olive oil and herbs.

Sous Vide Asparagus

Ingredients:

- 1 bunch asparagus, trimmed
- 1 tbsp olive oil
- Salt and pepper to taste
- 1 tbsp lemon juice (optional)

Instructions:

1. Preheat the sous vide water bath to 85°C (185°F).
2. Season asparagus with olive oil, salt, and pepper, and optionally add lemon juice.
3. Vacuum seal the asparagus in a bag.
4. Cook for 15-20 minutes in the water bath until tender.
5. Remove from the bag and serve immediately, garnished with extra lemon or herbs.

Sous Vide Potatoes

Ingredients:

- 4 medium potatoes, peeled and cubed
- 2 tbsp olive oil
- 2 cloves garlic, minced
- 1 tbsp rosemary, chopped
- Salt and pepper to taste

Instructions:

1. Preheat the sous vide water bath to 85°C (185°F).
2. Toss potatoes in olive oil, garlic, rosemary, salt, and pepper.
3. Vacuum seal the potatoes in a bag.
4. Cook for 1 to 1.5 hours in the water bath until soft.
5. Remove from the bag, then toss in a hot skillet for a few minutes to crisp them up, or serve immediately.

Sous Vide Carrots

Ingredients:

- 6 large carrots, peeled and sliced
- 1 tbsp butter
- 1 tbsp honey (optional)
- Salt and pepper to taste

Instructions:

1. Preheat the sous vide water bath to 85°C (185°F).
2. Season carrots with butter, honey, salt, and pepper.
3. Vacuum seal the carrots in a bag.
4. Cook for 45-60 minutes in the water bath until tender.
5. Serve immediately as a sweet and savory side.

Sous Vide Sweet Potatoes

Ingredients:

- 2 large sweet potatoes, peeled and cubed
- 1 tbsp olive oil
- 1 tsp cinnamon
- 1 tbsp maple syrup (optional)
- Salt to taste

Instructions:

1. Preheat the sous vide water bath to 85°C (185°F).
2. Toss sweet potatoes with olive oil, cinnamon, maple syrup, and salt.
3. Vacuum seal the sweet potatoes in a bag.
4. Cook for 1.5 to 2 hours in the water bath until soft.
5. Remove from the bag and serve as a side or mashed with a bit of butter.

Sous Vide Corn on the Cob

Ingredients:

- 4 ears of corn, husked
- 1 tbsp butter
- Salt and pepper to taste

Instructions:

1. Preheat the sous vide water bath to 85°C (185°F).
2. Coat the corn with butter, salt, and pepper.
3. Vacuum seal the corn in a bag.
4. Cook for 45 minutes to 1 hour in the water bath until tender.
5. Remove from the bag and serve with additional butter and seasoning.

Sous Vide Eggs (Soft/Hard Boiled)

Ingredients:

- 6 eggs (or more, as needed)

Instructions:

1. Preheat the sous vide water bath to 63°C (145°F) for soft-boiled or 68°C (154°F) for hard-boiled.
2. Carefully place the eggs directly into the water bath.
3. Cook for 45 minutes for soft-boiled or 1 hour for hard-boiled eggs.
4. Once done, remove the eggs and immediately place them in an ice bath for 2 minutes to stop the cooking process.
5. Peel and serve immediately or refrigerate for later use.

Sous Vide Scallops

Ingredients:

- 12 large scallops, cleaned
- 2 tbsp butter
- Salt and pepper to taste
- 1 tbsp lemon juice (optional)
- 1 sprig fresh thyme (optional)

Instructions:

1. Preheat the sous vide water bath to 50°C (122°F).
2. Season scallops with salt, pepper, and butter. Optionally add lemon juice and thyme.
3. Vacuum seal the scallops in a bag.
4. Cook for 30 minutes in the water bath.
5. Once done, quickly sear the scallops in a hot pan for 30 seconds to 1 minute on each side. Serve immediately.

Sous Vide Cheesecake

Ingredients:

- 500g cream cheese, softened
- 200g granulated sugar
- 2 large eggs
- 1 tsp vanilla extract
- 200g digestive biscuits (for the crust)
- 100g melted butter

Instructions:

1. Preheat the sous vide water bath to 80°C (176°F).
2. Crush the digestive biscuits and mix with melted butter. Press into the bottom of a mason jar or a silicone baking mold.
3. In a bowl, beat cream cheese, sugar, eggs, and vanilla until smooth. Pour the mixture into the jars over the crust.
4. Seal the jars and place them in the water bath.
5. Cook for 1 to 1.5 hours, then remove from the bath and let them cool to room temperature before refrigerating for at least 4 hours.
6. Serve chilled with your favorite toppings such as fruit or whipped cream.

Sous Vide Ribs

Ingredients:

- 1 rack baby back ribs
- 2 tbsp BBQ rub
- 1 cup BBQ sauce
- 1 tbsp olive oil

Instructions:

1. Preheat sous vide water bath to **74°C (165°F) for 12 hours** or **65°C (149°F) for 24 hours** (longer time = more tender ribs).
2. Season ribs with BBQ rub and vacuum seal.
3. Cook in the sous vide bath for the chosen time.
4. Remove, pat dry, and brush with BBQ sauce.
5. Sear on a hot grill or under the broiler for 3-5 minutes.

Sous Vide Chicken Wings

Ingredients:

- 1 kg chicken wings
- 1 tbsp olive oil
- 1 tsp garlic powder
- 1 tsp paprika
- Salt and pepper to taste
- ½ cup buffalo or BBQ sauce

Instructions:

1. Preheat sous vide water bath to **74°C (165°F) for 1.5 hours**.
2. Toss wings with oil, garlic powder, paprika, salt, and pepper.
3. Vacuum seal and cook.
4. Remove, pat dry, and broil or air-fry at 220°C (425°F) for 5-10 minutes.
5. Toss in sauce before serving.

Sous Vide Brisket

Ingredients:

- 1.5 kg beef brisket
- 2 tbsp salt
- 2 tbsp black pepper
- 1 tbsp garlic powder
- 1 tbsp smoked paprika

Instructions:

1. Preheat sous vide water bath to **68°C (155°F) for 24 hours**.
2. Rub brisket with salt, pepper, garlic powder, and paprika.
3. Vacuum seal and cook.
4. Remove, pat dry, and sear in a hot skillet or grill for 2-3 minutes per side.
5. Slice and serve with BBQ sauce.

Sous Vide Steak Frites

Ingredients:

- 2 ribeye or New York strip steaks
- Salt and pepper
- 2 tbsp butter
- 2 cloves garlic
- 2 sprigs thyme
- 2 large potatoes, cut into fries

Instructions:

1. Preheat sous vide water bath to **54°C (130°F) for medium-rare**.
2. Season steaks and vacuum seal with butter, garlic, and thyme.
3. Cook for 1.5-2 hours.
4. Remove, pat dry, and sear in a hot skillet for 1-2 minutes per side.
5. Serve with crispy fries cooked separately.

Sous Vide Crab Cakes

Ingredients:

- 500g crab meat
- ½ cup breadcrumbs
- 1 egg
- 2 tbsp mayonnaise
- 1 tsp Dijon mustard
- 1 tbsp lemon juice
- 1 tsp Old Bay seasoning

Instructions:

1. Preheat sous vide water bath to **60°C (140°F)**.
2. Mix all ingredients and shape into crab cakes.
3. Place in a vacuum bag in a single layer and cook for 45 minutes.
4. Remove and sear in a hot pan for 1-2 minutes per side.

Sous Vide Pork Chops

Ingredients:

- 2 thick-cut pork chops
- Salt and pepper
- 1 tbsp butter
- 1 sprig rosemary

Instructions:

1. Preheat sous vide water bath to **60°C (140°F) for juicy chops**.
2. Season pork and vacuum seal with butter and rosemary.
3. Cook for 1.5-2 hours.
4. Remove, pat dry, and sear for 1-2 minutes per side in a hot pan.

Sous Vide Beef Wellington

Ingredients:

- 500g beef tenderloin
- 1 tbsp salt
- 1 tbsp black pepper
- 2 tbsp Dijon mustard
- 100g mushrooms, finely chopped
- 4 slices prosciutto
- 1 sheet puff pastry
- 1 egg (for egg wash)

Instructions:

1. Preheat sous vide water bath to **54°C (130°F) for medium-rare**.
2. Season beef and vacuum seal. Cook for 1.5 hours.
3. Remove, pat dry, and sear quickly in a hot pan.
4. Spread Dijon mustard over the beef, then wrap in mushrooms and prosciutto.
5. Wrap in puff pastry, brush with egg wash, and bake at 200°C (400°F) for 15-20 minutes.

Sous Vide Banana Bread

Ingredients:

- 2 ripe bananas, mashed
- 100g sugar
- 100g butter, melted
- 2 eggs
- 1 tsp vanilla extract
- 200g all-purpose flour
- 1 tsp baking soda
- ½ tsp salt

Instructions:

1. Preheat sous vide water bath to **85°C (185°F)**.
2. Mix ingredients and pour batter into mason jars.
3. Seal the jars loosely and cook in the water bath for 2 hours.
4. Let cool and serve.

Sous Vide Oysters

Ingredients:

- 6 fresh oysters
- 2 tbsp butter
- 1 tsp garlic, minced
- 1 tbsp lemon juice

Instructions:

1. Preheat sous vide water bath to **48°C (118°F)**.
2. Shuck the oysters and place them in vacuum bags with butter, garlic, and lemon juice.
3. Cook for 20-30 minutes.
4. Serve immediately with fresh herbs.

Sous Vide Fried Chicken

Ingredients:

- 4 bone-in, skin-on chicken thighs or breasts
- 1 cup buttermilk
- 1 tbsp hot sauce (optional)
- 1 cup all-purpose flour
- 1 tsp paprika
- 1 tsp garlic powder
- 1 tsp salt
- ½ tsp black pepper
- ½ tsp cayenne pepper (optional)
- Vegetable oil for frying

Instructions:

1. Preheat sous vide water bath to **74°C (165°F)**.
2. Season chicken with salt and pepper, then vacuum seal with buttermilk and hot sauce.
3. Cook for **2 hours**, then remove and pat dry.
4. Mix flour, paprika, garlic powder, salt, black pepper, and cayenne in a bowl.
5. Dredge chicken in the flour mixture, then fry in 180°C (350°F) oil for **2-3 minutes** until crispy.

Sous Vide Meatballs

Ingredients:

- 500g ground beef or pork
- ½ cup breadcrumbs
- 1 egg
- 2 tbsp Parmesan cheese, grated
- 1 tsp garlic powder
- 1 tsp dried oregano
- Salt and pepper to taste

Instructions:

1. Preheat sous vide water bath to **63°C (145°F) for tender meatballs**.
2. Mix all ingredients and form into small meatballs.
3. Place in a vacuum-sealed bag in a single layer.
4. Cook for **1.5 to 2 hours**.
5. Remove and sear in a hot pan or broil for a few minutes before serving with marinara sauce.

Sous Vide Venison

Ingredients:

- 2 venison steaks (or backstrap)
- 1 tbsp olive oil
- 1 clove garlic, minced
- 1 sprig rosemary
- Salt and pepper to taste

Instructions:

1. Preheat sous vide water bath to **54°C (130°F) for medium-rare**.
2. Season venison with salt, pepper, olive oil, garlic, and rosemary.
3. Vacuum seal and cook for **1.5 to 2 hours**.
4. Remove, pat dry, and sear for **1-2 minutes per side** in a hot pan with butter.

Sous Vide Duck Confit

Ingredients:

- 2 duck legs
- 1 cup duck fat
- 2 cloves garlic, crushed
- 1 sprig thyme
- 1 tsp salt
- ½ tsp black pepper

Instructions:

1. Preheat sous vide water bath to **77°C (170°F)**.
2. Season duck legs with salt and pepper, then vacuum seal with duck fat, garlic, and thyme.
3. Cook for **12-24 hours**.
4. Remove, pat dry, and crisp skin in a hot pan for **3-5 minutes** before serving.

Sous Vide Pork Ribs

Ingredients:

- 1 rack baby back ribs
- 2 tbsp BBQ rub
- 1 cup BBQ sauce

Instructions:

1. Preheat sous vide water bath to **65°C (149°F) for 24 hours** or **74°C (165°F) for 12 hours**.
2. Season ribs with BBQ rub and vacuum seal.
3. Cook for chosen time.
4. Remove, pat dry, and brush with BBQ sauce.
5. Broil or grill for **5-10 minutes** until caramelized.

Sous Vide Gnocchi

Ingredients:

- 500g potatoes, boiled and mashed
- 1 cup all-purpose flour
- 1 egg
- 1 tsp salt

Instructions:

1. Preheat sous vide water bath to **85°C (185°F)**.
2. Mix mashed potatoes, flour, egg, and salt into a dough.
3. Roll into ropes, cut into gnocchi pieces, and vacuum seal.
4. Cook for **45 minutes**, then sear in a pan with butter before serving.

Sous Vide Pork Ragu

Ingredients:

- 500g pork shoulder, cubed
- 1 onion, chopped
- 2 cloves garlic, minced
- 1 can (400g) crushed tomatoes
- 1 tsp oregano
- 1 tsp salt
- ½ tsp black pepper

Instructions:

1. Preheat sous vide water bath to **75°C (167°F)**.
2. Mix all ingredients and vacuum seal.
3. Cook for **24 hours**.
4. Remove, shred pork, and mix with sauce.
5. Serve over pasta.

Sous Vide Eggplant Parmesan

Ingredients:

- 1 large eggplant, sliced into ½-inch rounds
- 1 tsp salt
- 1 cup marinara sauce
- ½ cup mozzarella cheese, shredded
- ¼ cup Parmesan cheese, grated
- 1 cup breadcrumbs
- 1 egg, beaten
- 1 tbsp olive oil

Instructions:

1. Preheat sous vide water bath to **85°C (185°F)**.
2. Sprinkle salt over eggplant slices and let sit for 15 minutes to remove moisture. Pat dry.
3. Dip slices in beaten egg, then coat with breadcrumbs.
4. Vacuum seal eggplant slices in a single layer and cook for **1 hour**.
5. Remove, place slices in a baking dish, top with marinara sauce and cheese, and broil for **5 minutes** until golden and bubbly.

Sous Vide Beef Bolognese

Ingredients:

- 500g ground beef
- 1 onion, chopped
- 2 cloves garlic, minced
- 1 can (400g) crushed tomatoes
- ½ cup red wine
- 1 tsp oregano
- 1 tsp basil
- Salt and pepper to taste

Instructions:

1. Preheat sous vide water bath to **75°C (167°F)**.
2. Brown the beef in a pan, then drain excess fat.
3. Mix all ingredients in a vacuum-sealed bag.
4. Cook in the water bath for **12 hours**.
5. Serve over pasta with Parmesan cheese.

Sous Vide Caramelized Onions

Ingredients:

- 2 large onions, thinly sliced
- 2 tbsp butter
- 1 tsp salt
- 1 tsp sugar

Instructions:

1. Preheat sous vide water bath to **85°C (185°F)**.
2. Mix onions with butter, salt, and sugar in a vacuum bag.
3. Cook for **12 hours**.
4. Use in sandwiches, burgers, or as a side dish.

Sous Vide Tofu

Ingredients:

- 1 block firm tofu, cut into cubes

- 2 tbsp soy sauce
- 1 tbsp sesame oil
- 1 tsp garlic powder
- 1 tsp ginger powder

Instructions:

1. Preheat sous vide water bath to **85°C (185°F)**.
2. Marinate tofu with soy sauce, sesame oil, garlic, and ginger.
3. Vacuum seal and cook for **1 hour**.
4. Remove and crisp up in a skillet for **3-5 minutes** if desired.

Sous Vide Grilled Cheese Sandwich

Ingredients:

- 2 slices bread
- 2 tbsp butter
- 100g cheese (cheddar, gouda, or mozzarella)

Instructions:

1. Preheat sous vide water bath to **75°C (167°F)**.
2. Butter both sides of the bread and place cheese between them.
3. Vacuum seal carefully (do not over-compress).
4. Cook for **30-45 minutes**.
5. Remove and sear in a skillet for **2-3 minutes per side** until golden brown.

Sous Vide Risotto

Ingredients:

- 1 cup Arborio rice
- 2 cups chicken or vegetable broth
- ½ cup white wine
- ½ cup Parmesan cheese, grated
- 1 tbsp butter
- ½ tsp salt

Instructions:

1. Preheat sous vide water bath to **85°C (185°F)**.
2. Combine rice, broth, wine, salt, and butter in a vacuum bag.
3. Cook for **45 minutes to 1 hour**, massaging the bag halfway through.
4. Stir in Parmesan cheese before serving.

Sous Vide Apple Pie

Ingredients:

For the filling:

- 3 apples, peeled and sliced
- ¼ cup sugar
- 1 tsp cinnamon
- 1 tbsp butter

For the crust:

- 1 sheet pie dough

Instructions:

1. Preheat sous vide water bath to **85°C (185°F)**.
2. Vacuum seal apples, sugar, cinnamon, and butter in a bag.
3. Cook for **1 hour** until soft.
4. Fill a pre-baked pie crust with the apple mixture and bake for **10 minutes** at 180°C (350°F) to crisp up the crust.

www.ingramcontent.com/pod-product-compliance
Lightning Source LLC
LaVergne TN
LVHW081509060526
838201LV00056BA/3018